SME TO SME

*Journey from being a **Small & Medium Enterprise** to a **Systematically Managed Enterprise***

SME TO SME

*Journey from being a **Small & Medium Enterprise** to a **Systematically Managed Enterprise***

CA Vikash Jain

Worldwide Published by

Pendown Press

PENDOWN PRESS LLP

An ISO 9001 & ISO 14001 Certified Co.,

Regd. Office: 3767A, Kanhaiya Nagar,

Tri Nagar, Delhi-110035

Ph.: 8130886000, 9650072927, 8595249536

E-mail: info@pendownpress.com

Branch Office: 1A/2A, 20, Hari Sadan, Ansari Road,

Daryaganj, New Delhi-110002

Ph.: 011-45794768

Website: PendownPress.com

Edition: 2025

ISBN: 978-93-6338-347-0

Layout and Cover Designed by Pendown Graphics Team
Printed and Bound in India by Thomson Press India Ltd.

Dedication

To My Beloved City of Durgapur. To the city that shaped me—my birthplace and workplace - Durgapur, the vibrant heart of West Bengal's SME ecosystem. Your industrial spirit, resilient entrepreneurs, and hardworking people have taught me everything I know about business and perseverance. From your steel plants to your small workshops, you embody the spirit of enterprise and transformation.

To the Dreamers and the Doers!

To the visionaries who dared to transform — Sri Kabi Dutta, Sri Arunangshu Ganguly, Sri Deepak Agarwal, Sri Vinay Agarwal, Smt. Radha Bhattad, Sri Amit Chatterjee, and countless others who showed us that the journey from a Small and Medium Enterprise to a Systematically Managed Enterprise is not just a dream, but an achievable reality. Your stories light the way.

To every entrepreneur who rises before dawn and works past dusk, wrestling with challenges, balancing dreams with reality, and working tirelessly to build something meaningful — This book is for you.

May these pages light your path from survival to success, from chaos to system, from managing to leading.

Your struggles inspired this book. Your determination fuels its purpose. Your future success will be its greatest reward.

Remember: Every great enterprise began as someone's dream and grew through someone's determination. Your journey matters. Your transformation awaits.

And like Durgapur itself — Where small workshops grew into industrial giants, Where entrepreneurial dreams found fertile soil — May your enterprise grow from strength to strength, From small to systematic, From local to legendary.

Table of Contents

Acknowledgement — i

Foreword - Dr Arunangshu Ganguly — iii

Foreword - Radha Sarda Bhattad — v

Foreword - CA Parinita Adukia — vii

Foreword - Amit Chatterjee — viii

Meet Your Author — ix

Preface — xi

- **Chapter 1** — 1
  The SME Journey:
  From Survival to Success

- **Chapter 2** — 6
  Building the Business of Your Dreams -
  The Systematically Managed Enterprise

- **Chapter 3** — 12
  Transforming Your Mental Model -
  The Leadership Journey

- **Chapter 4** — 17
  Building Your Business Machine -
  The Systems That Set You Free

- **Chapter 5** — 23
  Building Your Dream Team -
  From Workers to Winners

- **Chapter 6** — 29
  From Customers to Champions -
  Building Your Brand Army

- **Chapter 7**   35
  The Symphony of Systems -
  Creating Your Business Orchestra

- **Chapter 8**   41
  The Heartbeat of Success -
  Leading with Vision

- **Chapter 9**   47
  The Money Map -
  Charting Your Financial Success

- **Chapter 10**   53
  Building Your Growth Machine -
  The Art of Scaling Smart

- **Chapter 11**   60
  Riding the AI Wave -
  Future-Proofing Your Business

- **Chapter 12**   66
  Embracing Change -
  From Resistance to Renaissance

- **Chapter 13**   72
  The Transformation Blueprint -
  Your Journey from Small to Systematic

- **Chapter 14**   78
  Your Living Legacy -
  Building Beyond Business

- **Words of Praise**   84

— Acknowledgements —

Every transformation journey begins with inspiration, and this book is no exception. As I reflect on the path that led to these pages, I am filled with gratitude for the many people who made this possible.

To **my mother,** who taught me my first lessons in systematic thinking and perseverance - your wisdom continues to guide me. Your belief in education and continuous improvement laid the foundation for who I am today.

To **my wife,** who has been my steadfast partner through every challenge and triumph - your unwavering support and understanding have made this journey possible. You've been both my anchor and my wings.

To **my daughter Khushi,** who not only inspires me to build a better future but also contributed significantly to this book - your insights and assistance have been invaluable. You represent the next generation of systematic thinkers who will carry these principles forward.

To **my brother, sister, and all my family members** - your constant encouragement and unconditional support have been a source of strength throughout this journey.

To **my partner Amit Khemka and the entire Jain Khemka & Associates family** - your unwavering support, dedication, and insightful contributions have been crucial to both my professional journey and this book. The way our team exemplifies systematic management in daily practice has added authenticity to many concepts discussed here, and your collective commitment to excellence continues to inspire me.

To my dear friend Deepak Chowdhury - your strategic thinking and practical insights have been instrumental in developing the concepts in this book. Your friendship and counsel have been gifts I deeply treasure.

To Amit Chatterjee - your blend of friendship and business acumen has contributed significantly to the practical approaches outlined in these pages. Your experiences and insights have added depth to many of the strategies discussed.

To all my clients in the SME sector - you are the heart of this book. Your struggles, challenges, and aspirations lit the fire that inspired me to write this guide. Your daily battles to grow your businesses, your resilience in the face of obstacles, and your dreams of building lasting institutions have been my greatest teachers.

To Dinesh Verma and the entire team at Pendown Press - your expertise, dedication, and meticulous attention to detail have been instrumental in bringing this book to life. Your tireless efforts in editing, designing, and shaping the manuscript have transformed my ideas into a polished final product. Your commitment to excellence has enhanced the book's ability to reach and impact its intended audience.

Finally, to every entrepreneur who picks up this book - your desire to transform your business from a Small and Medium Enterprise to a Systematically Managed Enterprise is what gives these pages purpose. Your journey continues to inspire me.

This book is not just a collection of ideas and strategies - it's a testament to the power of systematic transformation and the importance of having the right people beside you on the journey.

— *Foreword* —

The precise treatise is an absolute revelation to many entrepreneurs as to how simple interventions can make a sea change in the pursuit of their goals.

All entrepreneurs start their journey with a passion to do something different as to make a distinctive mark in their field or in the society.

They strive to achieve their version at all costs. In the process they all fall victims to their passion and vision ending up being a one-man army and crawl towards early burn out because the most important thing in life is lost – the balance. When giving time to work family suffers and the vice versa. Besides the work done also falls behind the ever - changing requirements and expectations.

While going through this simple, relaxed reading book the aroma of everyday reality mesmerised me, and the book was finished in one breath. Every page, every detail transported me through a déjà vu but when my brain started to work on the seemingly innocuous suggests and rich quotes and rhetorics, I realised the depth of knowledge impregnated in the flawless, simple, and deeply rooted to the ground narrative.

The book is a must read for anyone who remotely dreams of a venture of his own. It will inspire and guide them to apply the simple practices and correctives in their endeavour to culminate their passion and vision to "Absolute success" which simply be defined as "Achieving success while maintaining a proper work life balance". In this nail-biting competitive world this is a mirage which is the haunting silent killer of humanity.

Thank you, my friend and guide, for writing this beautiful piece. We earnestly look for more.

Dr Arunangshu Ganguly

MD DNB(Card) MNAMS FESC FACC FSCAI

Senior Interventional Cardiologist

CMD | Healthworld Hospitals.

It is both an honor and a privilege to write the foreword for a book authored by someone as extraordinary as Vikash Jee. For over two decades, Vikash Jee has not only been the pillar of financial expertise for our company but also a relentless planner, a strategist, and a visionary whose insights have consistently guided us toward sustainable growth and success.

Through his meticulous planning and sharp foresight, Vikash Jee has demonstrated time and again how thoughtful strategies can transform challenges into opportunities. His dedication to empowering businesses, especially in the SME sector, is unparalleled. With his deep understanding of business dynamics, Vikash Jee has been instrumental in helping enterprises like ours achieve financial discipline and strategic clarity.

Now, with "SME to SME," Vikash Jee extends his wisdom and expertise to a wider audience. This book is not just a guide; it is a roadmap for SMEs to unlock their true potential. It reflects his years of hands-on experience, his deep connection with the challenges and aspirations of SMEs, and his commitment to seeing them thrive in an ever-evolving business landscape.

I am confident that "SME to SME" will be a source of inspiration, knowledge, and actionable insights for entrepreneurs, professionals, and business leaders. Vikash Jee's unique ability to simplify complex concepts while providing practical solutions ensures that this book will leave a lasting impact on its readers.

As someone who has had the privilege of working closely with him for so many years, I can attest to the fact that this book encapsulates the essence of his wisdom and passion for helping businesses grow. I wholeheartedly recommend this book to anyone who wishes to elevate their SME journey to new heights.

Thank you, Vikash Jee, for sharing your invaluable experience with the world. I wish you and this book immense success.

With deep respect and admiration,

Radha Sarda Bhattad

Sunrise Movers & Carriers LLP

Foreword

It is my privilege to pen this foreword and introduce you to this remarkable work that promises to transform the way SMEs operate. The author, a seasoned Chartered Accountant with a wealth of experience in managing and mentoring SMEs, brings a unique perspective to this work.

Over the years, he has been at the forefront of guiding countless businesses toward financial discipline, compliance, and operational efficiency. What sets this book apart is not just its practical approach but also the clarity with which the author addresses complex challenges. With actionable insights, relatable examples, and a systematic framework, this book serves as a roadmap for SMEs striving to evolve into well-structured, future-ready organizations.

Through his rich experience, the author has identified the core principles that drive success for SMEs, and this book encapsulates his learnings in a manner that is both insightful and inspiring.

I am certain that this book will not only resonate with SME owners but will also serve as a valuable resource for aspiring entrepreneurs, professionals, and anyone invested in fostering the growth of this critical sector.

I congratulate the author on this significant contribution to the business community and encourage you to immerse yourself in the insights it offers.

CA Parinita Adukia

Foreword

While going through the book, I relived my journey that I travelled since 1992 from the enhancement of bank loans to rehabilitation, reconstruction to debt recovery tribunals.

Fire fighting every single day on all fronts trying to do everything by myself.

Until one day, a friend suggested me to meet CA Vikash Jain, the author of this book. My financial and commercial worries were completely taken care of, and I got some much needed time to think and improve on the lacunas of the business model, and slowly, we emerged successful in turning around the business and expand into new horizons.

I am confident that this book shall be like the much needed prescription to many struggling entrepreneurs making the same old mistakes, which I made at that time. I am sure reading the book they will also emerge successful without having to do fire fighting at all times.

Amit Chatterjee

Director Durgapur Tubes Pvt. Ltd.

CA Vikash Jain is a distinguished Chartered Accountant with over 24 years of expertise in auditing, taxation, and consulting. Since earning his CA qualification in 2000, he has established himself as a trusted advisor, mentor, and thought leader in the field of finance.

Driven by an unyielding passion for knowledge and innovation, he has enhanced his professional acumen through specialized courses from ICAI, covering areas such as Concurrent Audit of Banks, Real Estate, Artificial Intelligence, and Machine Learning. He has also expanded his understanding of technology and business leadership through a course on Artificial Intelligence from Be10X, the Business Mastery Program from Business Coaching India (Rahul Jain), and the Mastering Business with AI & Technology program by CEOITBOX (Sanjeev Jain).

In addition to his qualifications, CA Vikash Jain is deeply committed to sharing knowledge. He regularly conducts training sessions on GST, Income Tax, Audits, and the practical application of Artificial Intelligence and Automation tools for his team and clients. His sessions reflect his belief in empowering others to achieve excellence in their respective fields.

A staunch advocate for leveraging technology in business, he champions the integration of AI and automation to simplify processes, improve decision-making, and enhance efficiency. His forward-thinking approach is a testament to his ability to adapt and thrive in the ever-evolving landscape of business and technology.

Currently, he is channeling his decades of experience into authoring SME to SME: Journey from being a Small & Medium Enterprise to a

Systematically Managed Enterprise. This transformative book reflects his vision of helping businesses evolve into structured, scalable, and systematically managed enterprises.

Through his work, he aims to inspire entrepreneurs to reach their full potential and contribute to making India a hub of thriving, well-managed enterprises.

—— *Preface* ——

In my journey of over two decades as a Chartered Accountant and a business advisor, I have had the privilege of working closely with countless Small and Medium Enterprises (SMEs). These businesses are the lifeblood of economies, driving innovation, creating jobs, and fostering community development.

Yet, I have also witnessed the struggles many SMEs face—unstructured operations, financial mismanagement, and a lack of scalable systems that hinder their true potential.

This book—

"SME to SME – Journey from being a Small &
Medium Enterprise to a Systematically Managed Enterprise"

is born out of my deep desire to empower entrepreneurs like you to overcome these challenges.

It is not just a guide; it is a blueprint for transformation. It encapsulates lessons learned from real-world experiences, practical tools, and actionable strategies to help you scale your business and achieve sustainable growth.

The concept of transforming an SME from being just a "Small and Medium Enterprise" into a "Systematically Managed Enterprise" is more than a play on words—it is a shift in mindset.

It is about moving from reactive management to proactive leadership, from ad-hoc decisions to structured strategies, and from short-term survival to long-term success.

➢ This book is divided into 14 chapters, each designed to address a critical aspect of your business transformation.

- ➤ From building the right mindset and establishing robust systems to leveraging technology, fostering leadership, and creating a legacy, every chapter is packed with insights and practical advice to guide you at every step of your journey.

- ➤ This Book is meant for— Entrepreneurs, Manufacturers, Service Providers, Business Consultants, and anyone aspiring to professionalize and grow their business.

- ➤ Whether you are a budding entrepreneur or an experienced business owner, this book aims to equip you with the tools and perspective needed to unlock your business's true potential.

- ➤ By following the principles outlined here, you can not only grow your enterprise but also contribute to building a thriving ecosystem where businesses, employees, and communities flourish together.

As you embark on this transformative journey, remember that success is not just about the destination, but the process of growth and learning along the way. I am certain this book will serve as a trusted companion in your pursuit of excellence and inspire you to create a legacy that extends beyond profits.

Here's to building a future where every SME can thrive as a Systematically Managed Enterprise.

Warm regards,
CA Vikash Jain

□ □ □ □

Chapter - 1

The SME Journey:
From Survival to Success

Picture this: It's 10 PM, and you're still at your factory, reviewing quotations after spending the whole day managing workers, handling customer calls, and chasing payments. Sounds familiar? If you're an SME owner, you're probably nodding right now.

I've seen this scene play out countless times during my 25 years of working with small and medium enterprises in Durgapur. Whether it's the local steel fabricator working 14-hour days or the software company founder who hasn't taken a vacation in years – the story often starts the same way.

The Birth of a Dream

Remember why you started? Maybe it was that burning desire to create something of your own. Perhaps you saw a market opportunity that nobody else did, or maybe it was simply the dream of building a legacy for your family.

Today, you're part of a powerful force that contributes 30% to India's GDP and employs over 155 million people.
But statistics don't tell the entire story, do they?

The Reality Behind the Numbers

"Last night, my daughter asked me when I would attend her annual day function. I promised 'next year' – for the third time in a row," shared Vinay, a client who runs a successful auto parts manufacturing unit. His story echoes what thousands of SME owners experience: the constant juggling act between business demands and their personal lives.

"You do not rise to the level of your goals.
You fall to the level of your systems."
— *James Clear, Atomic Habits*

This truth resonates deeply with every SME owner I've met. Your success isn't just about your dreams or hard work – it's about the systems you build to support those dreams.

The Common Threads

In my interactions with hundreds of business owners, I've noticed patterns that bind most SMEs together:

➢ You're the first one in and the last one out

➢ Every decision, big or small, needs your input

➢ Your phone never stops ringing with "urgent" matters

➢ Personal and business finances often blur together

➢ Growth feels like a double-edged sword – exciting but scary

The Seven Struggles Every SME Owner Knows Too Well

1. **The "Everything Is in My Head" Syndrome:** Ritesh's business came to a standstill when his father suddenly died due to COVID-19. Why? Because only his father knew where everything was, whom

to contact, and how things worked. "I realized then that being irreplaceable isn't a good thing," he told me.

2. **The Cash Flow Tightrope:** "I have orders worth 500 lakhs, but I can't sleep because I need to arrange 25 lakhs for tomorrow's salary payment." - This confession from Navneet, a manufacturing unit owner represents a common paradox. Growth brings bigger orders but also bigger financial challenges.

3. **The One-Person Orchestra:** You're the CEO, CFO, HR manager, and sometimes even the office boy. While this hands-on approach works initially, it eventually becomes your biggest growth barrier.

4. **The Technology Gap:** "My competitors have fancy software, but I'm comfortable with my notebooks," said a distributor in Durgapur. Six months later, he lost three major clients to a more tech-savvy competitor.

5. **The Talent Trap:** Finding good people is hard; keeping them is harder. Without proper systems, you're constantly training new employees while watching the experienced ones leave.

6. **The Market Ceiling:** Many SME owners I work with hit an invisible ceiling in their market reach. They know they could sell more, but something holds them back – usually the fear that their current way of working won't support expansion.

7. **The Work-Life Imbalance:** "I'm making good money, but I haven't played with my kids in weeks." This statement from a successful food processor haunts me because it represents so many SME owners.

"What got you here won't get you there."
— *Marshall Goldsmith*

This powerful truth often hits home when SME owners realize that the practices that helped them grow initially might be the very things holding them back now.

The Turning Point

Take Raghav's story. His Labour Supply business was chaotic three years ago. Today, it runs smoothly even when he takes two weeks off. The difference? He shifted from being just a **Small and Medium Enterprise** to becoming a **Systematically Managed Enterprise.**

> "A journey of a thousand miles begins with a single step."
> — *Lao Tzu*

Like that first step you took when starting your business, the journey to becoming a Systematically Managed Enterprise begins with a single decision. The decision to change, to evolve, to grow beyond the limitations of the traditional SME model.

A Simple Self-Check

Before we dive deeper, ask yourself:

- When was the last time you had dinner with your family without business calls?
- Can your business run without you for a week?
- Do you know your exact profit on each product or service?
- Is your team clear about their roles without your constant guidance?
- Do you have time to think about growth, or are you stuck putting out fires?

The Path Forward

The challenges faced by SMEs, while significant, are not insurmountable. With proper guidance, many of these hurdles can be transformed into stepping stones for growth. This book will guide you on how to evolve from being a **Small and Medium Enterprise** to becoming a **Systematically Managed Enterprise.**

By embracing this model, you can:

➢ Create systems that work even when you're not there

➢ Build a team that thinks and acts independently

➢ Generate consistent profits and sustainable growth

➢ Find time for both business growth and personal life

Remember, every business giant today started as an SME. The difference lies not in how they started, but in how they grew.

Your journey from being a Small and Medium Enterprise to becoming a Systematically Managed Enterprise begins now.

In the chapters ahead, we'll explore practical, proven ways to transform your business from a one-person operation into a well-oiled machine. Together, we'll build a business that works for you, instead of you working for it.

□ □ □ □

Chapter - 2

Building the Business of Your Dreams:
The Systematically Managed Enterprise

Remember Vinay from our last chapter - the auto parts manufacturer who kept missing his daughter's school functions? Six months after we met, he called me with excitement in his voice:

"Yesterday, I attended my daughter's dance recital. The factory ran perfectly without me."

> "Don't wish it were easier. Wish you were better."
> *—Jim Rohn*

This quote perfectly captures Vinay's transformation journey. Instead of wishing his business would magically become easier to manage, he chose to build better systems. Today, let's explore what that really means.

From Chaos to Clarity

Last month, I visited two manufacturing units in Kolkata. Both started around the same time, had similar products, and had comparable turnovers. Yet, one owner hadn't taken a vacation in three years, while the other had just returned from a two-week family trip.

The difference? One was running a traditional SME; the other had evolved into a Systematically Managed Enterprise.

"A business that depends entirely on you is not a business.
It's a job - and not a very good one."
— *Michael Gerber, The E-Myth Revisited*

What Makes a Business Truly Systematic?

Think of your business as a symphony orchestra. In a traditional SME, you're playing all the instruments yourself - exhausting and limiting. In a Systematically Managed Enterprise, you're the conductor - guiding each section while they play their parts perfectly.

Let me share some real transformations I've witnessed:

1. **From Memory to Methods:** Take Radha's Logistics business for example. Earlier, every order specification lived in her head or scattered notes. One wrong order almost cost her, her biggest client. Today, her team handles orders through a simple digital system. "Now I sleep better," she says, "knowing nothing will slip through the cracks."

2. **From One Brain to Many Minds:** "I used to be the answer man," laughs Arun, who runs a successful multi-specialty Hospital. "Every decision needed my approval. Now my team makes 80% of daily decisions using our documented guidelines. They often make better choices than I would!"

3. **From Gut Feel to Data-Driven:** When Deepak started tracking his manufacturing costs systematically, he discovered that his 'most profitable' product was actually losing money. "Data showed us the truth our instincts had missed," he admits.

The Six Pillars of Systematic Management

1. **Documented Wisdom:** Think of SOPs (Standard Operating Procedures) as your business recipe book. When Mohan's chief technician suddenly left, his machine maintenance didn't suffer - because every process was documented. New staff could step in seamlessly.

2. **Independent Operations:** "Business shouldn't stop because you caught a cold," I often tell my clients. Like Vinay's auto parts unit, your business should run smoothly even when you're not there.

3. **Financial Clarity:** "I now know my exact costs, margins, and cash position daily," shares Deepak, a steel manufacturer. "No more sleepless nights wondering if I can meet payroll."

4. **Smart Technology:** You don't need fancy software - just the right tools used well. A simple WhatsApp Business account helped Meena's spice business manage orders better. She later graduated to a basic ERP system as she grew.

5. **Growth-Ready Systems:** "We designed our processes thinking big," says Raghav, whose Labour Supply business grew from 500 to 2500 employees in two years. "What works for 10 orders should work for 100."

6. **People Development:** "Earlier, I hired hands. Now I develop minds," reflects Arun, the hospital owner. His investment in training created a team that thinks and solves problems independently.

The Real Benefits I've Seen

1. **Time Freedom:** "Last Sunday was the first time I played cricket with my son in years," shared a beaming client whose business now runs on systems.

2. **Consistent Quality:** A food processing unit reduced customer complaints by 70% within three months of implementing standard processes.

3. **Better Finances:** One of my clients secured a sizeable bank loan easily because his systematic operations impressed the bankers. "They could see we weren't just running a business; we were building an institution," he sayss.

What's Stopping You?

In my experience, these are the most common hurdles:

1. **The Control Trap:** "What if they make mistakes?" asks every business owner. My response: "They will. But wouldn't you rather have them make small mistakes now than have your business completely dependent on you forever?"

2. **The Cost Myth:** "I can't afford systems right now," said a client. Six months later: "I couldn't afford NOT to have systems. The wastage and inefficiencies were costing me more."

3. **The Comfort Zone:** Change is uncomfortable. But remember what happened to that distributor from Chapter 1 who was "comfortable" with his notebooks?

Taking Your First Steps

"The best time to plant a tree was 20 years ago.
The second best time is now."
— ***Chinese Proverb***

Here's how to begin:

1. **Start Small:** Begin with one process - maybe your order management or customer complaints. Document it, systematize it, perfect it.

2. **Build Gradually:** Don't try to transform everything overnight. Pick your battles. One client started by simply standardizing how phone calls were answered. Today, his entire business runs on systems.

3. **Involve Your Team:** Your employees often know what needs fixing. One owner was surprised when his workers suggested a better inventory management system than the expensive one he was considering.

Looking Ahead

In our next chapter, we'll explore the crucial mindset shifts needed to lead this transformation.

You'll learn how successful SME owners changed their thinking from "I must control everything" to "I must create systems for everything."

We'll dive deep into practical examples of how various business owners made this mental transition and the dramatic results they achieved.

Remember, every business that you admire today - from the largest corporations to the most efficient local enterprises - reached there by implementing systems. Your journey to becoming a Systematically Managed Enterprise starts with a single step. Are you ready to take that step?

How about starting by picking just one area of your business that you'd like to systematize? Think about it, and in the next chapter, we'll help you develop the mindset to make it happen.

Chapter - 3

Transforming Your Mental Model:
The Leadership Journey

"When was the last time you worked ON your business versus IN your business?"

This was the question I asked Ganesh, owner of a real estate business, who hadn't taken a single day off in three years. He looked puzzled, then smiled sadly. "I can't remember," he said. Six months later, he was spending three days a week strategizing growth while his team handled operations.

What changed? Not his business - his mindset.

"You can do anything, but not everything."
— *David Allen*

The Power of Perspective

Remember the two manufacturing units I visited in Kolkata last month? Same market, and similar turnover, yet drastically different lives. One worked 14-hour days, constantly firefighting issues. The other worked six hours a day, focusing mainly on strategy and growth.

The difference? How they thought about their role as business owners.

"Your business is a reflection of who you are."
— Michael Gerber

Five Critical Mindset Shifts I've Witnessed

1. **From Superman to Coach:** Purnendu, a Hotel owner, used to pride himself on being the first to arrive and last to leave. "Nobody can do it as well as me," he'd say. Today, he laughs at his old mindset.

   "I was the biggest obstacle to my growth," he admits. "Now I spend my time coaching my team rather than doing everything myself. Guess what? They often come up with better solutions than I would have!"

2. **From Firefighter to Architect:** "Every day was an emergency," recalls Subroto, who runs an educational institution. "I was constantly putting out fires. Then my mentor asked me a simple question: 'Would you rather spend your life fighting fires or building a fireproof building?'"

   Today, Subroto's morning starts with strategic planning, not crisis management. His team handles operational issues using well-documented processes.

3. **From Controller to Enabler:** "Letting go was my biggest fear," shares Vinay, whose auto parts business struggled until he changed his approach. "I thought control meant checking everything personally. Now I realize control comes from having robust systems and empowered people."

4. **From Short-Term Survivor to Long-Term Visionary:** Radha's Logistics business was profitable but stuck. "I was so focused on monthly targets that I couldn't see the bigger picture," she says. "When I started thinking in terms of years instead of months, everything changed. We invested in automation that initially seemed expensive but doubled our productivity within a year."

5. **From Gut Feel to Data-Driven:** "Data feels cold and impersonal," said Arun when I first suggested implementing analytics in his hospital. Six months later: "Numbers tell stories I would've never known. We discovered our most profitable product line wasn't what we thought it was!"

The Mental Blocks I Often Encounter

1. **The Perfectionist's Trap:** "Nobody will care about quality like I do," insisted Nitesh, a precision parts manufacturer. Today, his quality metrics are better than ever - managed by his well-trained team while he focuses on market expansion.

2. **The Busy Badge of Honour:** "I'm so busy" used to be Kanchan's proud response to every question. Now he knows better: "Being busy isn't the same as being productive. I accomplish more in 6 focused hours than I did in 12 hectic ones."

3. **The Money Mindset:** "We can't afford systems right now," is something I hear often. As one client realized: "The real question was: Could we afford to continue without systems? The answer was No."

Breaking Through: Practical Steps

1. **Start Your Day Differently:** Instead of jumping into operational work, spend your first hour thinking about your business's future. As one client says, "This one change revolutionized how I run my company."

2. **The Delegation Diary:** Keep a notebook. Every time you do something, ask: "Should I be doing this?" If the answer is no, write it down. At week's end, plan how to delegate these tasks.

3. **The Three Questions: Every evening, ask yourself:**

    - Did I work on my business today, or just in it?

    - Did I empower someone to make decisions?

    - Did I move closer to my long-term vision?

"When you change the way you look at things,
the things you look at change."
— *Wayne Dyer*

The Power of Community

One of the most effective mindset shifts I've seen happened through our local SME owner's group. Hearing others' transformation stories made change feel possible. As one member put it, "Seeing someone just like me succeed gave me the confidence to change."

Your Personal Transformation Plan

Start with these simple but powerful steps:

1. **Morning Vision Time:** Spend 30 minutes every morning envisioning your ideal business. What does it look like when it runs smoothly without your constant involvement?

2. **The Trust Exercise:** Each week, identify one decision you usually make and delegate it to a team member. Provide guidance, then step back.

3. **The Learning Commitment:** Dedicate time each week to learn about leadership and systems thinking. One client reads for 30 minutes every morning before setting foot in his factory.

Looking Ahead

In our next chapter, we'll explore how to turn these mindset shifts into practical systems.

You'll learn exactly how successful SME owners created their first standard operating procedure, what worked, what didn't, and how they built the foundation for systematic operations.

Remember, every business giant started with a leader who dared to think differently. Your journey to becoming a systematically managed enterprise isn't just about changing your business - it's about evolving as a leader.

As one of my most successful clients often says, "The day I decided to become a business leader instead of a business owner was the day my real growth began."

Are you ready to make that decision?

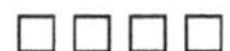

Chapter - 4

Building Your Business Machine: The Systems That Set You Free

"I spent fifteen years building a prison, and six months building an escape route."

These words from Vinay, a successful auto parts manufacturer, perfectly capture what many SME owners discover. The 'prison' he referred to was the business that couldn't run without him. The 'escape route'? The systems and processes we're about to explore.

"Standardization doesn't stifle creativity —
it sets the stage for innovation."

— Michael Gerber

Let's see how successful SME owners built their escape routes.

The Four Pillars of Freedom

1. **The Process Revolution:** Remember Radha's Logistics business? Orders were getting mixed up, deadlines were being missed, and she was constantly apologizing to customers. Today, her unit handles triple the volume with fewer errors. Her secret?

    "I finally understood that documenting processes isn't about creating bureaucracy—it's about creating freedom," she says.

Here's how she did it:

First Steps to Process Mastery:

➢ Start with your most painful process (for Radha, it was order processing)

➢ Document exactly how it's done now

➢ Ask your team: "What slows you down the most?"

➢ Create a simple, clear procedure everyone can follow

➢ Test, refine, and repeat

"My staff thought I was crazy when I spent three days just watching and documenting how we handle orders," Radha laughs. "Now they come to me with suggestions for improving our processes."

2. **The Money Map:** "I was making sales but losing money," admits Nitesh, who runs a precision parts unit. "I didn't know which products were actually profitable and which were eating up my resources."

Today, Nitesh's financial systems are so robust that he knows the exact costs and margins on every product. Here's his advice:

The Financial Foundation:

➢ Start with basic expense tracking (Nitesh began with a simple Excel sheet)

➢ Separate personal and business accounts (a step he wishes he'd taken years earlier)

➢ Track cash flow weekly (not monthly)

➢ Know your numbers: cost per unit, margins per product, monthly fixed costs

➢ Keep a three-month cash reserve (it saved his business during a major market downturn)

"The best investment I made wasn't in machinery—it was in my accounting software and training my accountant," Nitesh shares.

3. The Technology Transform:

"The world is changing fast. Big will not beat small anymore. It will be the fast beating the slow."
— *Rupert Murdoch*

This quote resonated deeply with Seema, who runs an Agro unit.

"I was resistant to technology," she admits. "Now I can't imagine running my business without it."

Her Tech Journey:
- Started with WhatsApp Business for customer orders (free and easy)
- Moved to basic accounting software (reduced errors by 90%)
- Added inventory management system (no more stockouts)
- Implemented CRM (customer relationships improved dramatically)
- Finally integrated everything with an ERP system

"Don't try to digitize everything at once," Seema advises. "Pick your biggest pain point and solve that first."

4. The People Puzzle:

"Alone we can do so little; together we can do so much."
— *Helen Keller*

"I used to think defining roles was too formal for our small business," says Amit, whose engineering unit now employs 500 people.

"Then I realized unclear roles create unclear results."

Building Your A-Team:

- Create clear job descriptions (Amit started with just three key positions)

- Define who's responsible for what (his favorite question: "Who owns this?")

- Set measurable goals for each role

- Create simple reporting structures

- Regular performance reviews (monthly, not yearly)

Real Results: The Freedom Formula

Let me share three transformation stories:

1. **The 2-Hour Owner:** Nitesh's Precision parts unit used to consume 12 hours of his day. After implementing these systems, he spends just two hours daily on the business, focusing purely on strategy and growth. "The business runs better without my constant interference," he admits.

2. **The Growth Story:** Mohit's retail trade grew 200% in two years after implementing proper systems. "Earlier, growth scared me because I couldn't handle current operations. Now my systems can scale infinitely."

3. **The Life Changer:** "Last month, I attended my son's school function for the first time in five years," shares Mahesh, a metal fabrication unit owner. "My systems and team handled everything while I was away."

Your Action Plan

Start Here:

1. **Process Mapping Week**
   - Pick one critical process
   - Document every step
   - Identify bottlenecks
   - Create a simple SOP
   - Test and refine

2. **Financial Clarity Month**
   - Upgrade your accounting software
   - Separate personal and business accounts
   - Track daily income and expenses
   - Calculate product-wise profitability
   - Set up weekly financial reviews

3. **Technology Integration Quarter**
   - List all manual, time-consuming tasks
   - Research simple software solutions
   - Start with one tool
   - Train your team thoroughly
   - Add more tools gradually

4. **Team Structure Semester**
   - Write clear job descriptions
   - Define reporting relationships
   - Set measurable goals
   - Create training programs
   - Regular performance reviews

Common Pitfalls to Avoid:

- Trying to perfect everything before implementing
- Implementing too many changes at once
- Not involving your team in the process
- Choosing complex solutions when simple ones would work
- Forgetting to monitor and adjust systems

Looking Ahead

In our next chapter, we'll explore how to build a strong organizational culture that supports these systems. You'll learn how successful SME owners created teams that don't just follow processes but embrace and improve them.

Remember Vinay from our opening story? He recently told me, "The systems we built didn't just free me from my business prison—they gave my team the power to build something greater than I could have built alone."

Your journey to systematic management isn't about creating rigid rules—it's about building a business machine that runs smoothly, grows consistently, and eventually works without your constant presence.

Are you ready to start building your escape route?

Chapter - 5

Building Your Dream Team:
From Workers to Winners

"My employees aren't just workers anymore — they're the architects of our future."

These words from Amit, whose engineering unit in Durgapur transformed from a struggling workshop to a thriving enterprise, perfectly capture the essence of team building in a Systematically Managed Enterprise.

"A great organization is built on the shoulders of great people."
— Jim Collins

The People Revolution: Real Stories

1. **The Retention Mystery:** "I couldn't understand why good people kept leaving," shares Arun, who runs a successful hospital. **"We paid well, but something was missing." Today, his company has one of the highest retention rates** in the industry.

    Let's discover what changed.

    Building Your Talent Magnet:

    - Create clear growth paths (Arun maps out 3-year career plans for each role)

    - Offer learning opportunities (he sponsors relevant courses for team members)

23

- Build a positive work environment (his unit now has flexible timing options)
- Recognize and reward performance (monthly appreciation ceremonies)
- Provide competitive compensation (regular market surveys)

2. **The Onboarding Revolution:** Raghav, the Labour Supplier, solved his constant training problems with what he calls the ***"Buddy System."***

"Every new hire gets a mentor for three months," he explains. "It's transformed how quickly people become productive."

The First 30 Days Plan:
- **Day 1:** Company vision and culture introduction
- **Week 1:** Role-specific training with their buddy
- **Week 2-3:** Hands-on practice with supervision
- **Week 4:** Independent work with daily check-ins
- **Month-end:** First performance review and feedback

3. **The Accountability Breakthrough:** "People rise to your expectations," says Radha, whose logistics business struggled with quality issues until she implemented what she calls **"Ownership Circles."**

Creating Accountability Champions:
- Assign clear responsibilities (written job descriptions)
- Set measurable goals (weekly targets)
- Regular feedback sessions (bi-weekly one-on-ones)
- Celebrate wins (monthly recognition programs)
- Learn from failures (no-blame problem-solving sessions)

> "Teamwork is the ability to work together
> toward a common vision."
> — *Andrew Carnegie*

4. **The Innovation Engine:** Deepak's steel manufacturing unit was losing market share until he created what he calls **"Think Tank Thursdays."**

Fostering Innovation:

- Weekly innovation meetings (30 minutes, everyone participates)
- Implement one new idea every month
- Reward successful innovations (both financially and publicly)
- Learn from failed experiments
- Share success stories across departments

"Our best-selling product came from a machine operator's suggestion during Think Tank Thursday," Deepak proudly shares.

5. **The Learning Laboratory:**

> "Before you are a leader, success is all about growing yourself.
> When you become a leader, success is all about growing others."
> — *Jack Welch*

Ragav's labour supply business transformed when he started investing 5% of profits in employee development.

The Growth Blueprint:

- Technical skills training (monthly workshops)
- Soft skills development (quarterly programs)
- Leadership coaching (for potential managers)

- Cross-functional training (job rotation program)
- External certifications (company-sponsored)

"My best manager started as a shop floor worker," Raghav beams. "Education isn't about degrees—it's about the desire to learn."

Creating Your Culture Code

1. **The Vision Connection:** Vinay's auto components unit struggled until he made every employee understand their role in the company's success.

   Making Vision Visible:
   - Monthly town halls (company updates)
   - Department goal-setting sessions
   - Individual contribution maps
   - Success story sharing
   - Regular vision reinforcement

2. **The Recognition Revolution:** Ganesh's real estate business created a unique rewards system that transformed productivity.

   The Recognition Toolkit:
   - Monthly Star Performer awards
   - Quarterly team celebrations
   - Annual achievement ceremonies
   - Skill development opportunities
   - Family involvement programs

> **A Real Success Story: The Power of People**
>
> Let me share Radha's story. Her logistics business was struggling with high turnover and low morale. "I was the boss, but not a leader," she admits. After implementing systematic people development:
>
> - Employee turnover dropped by 80%
> - Productivity increased by 50%
> - The business expanded to multiple cities
> - Team size grew from 15 to 50
> - Customer satisfaction improved dramatically

Your Action Plan

Week 1: Talent Assessment

➢ Review current roles and responsibilities

➢ Identify skill gaps

➢ Create a training needs list

➢ Plan growth paths for key positions

Month 1: Culture Building

➢ Define your company values

➢ Create recognition programs

➢ Start regular team meetings

➢ Implement feedback systems

Quarter 1: Development Program

➢ Launch basic training modules

➢ Start mentorship program

➢ Implement performance reviews

➢ Create learning opportunities

Looking Ahead

In our next chapter, we'll explore how your empowered team can build stronger customer relationships.

You'll learn how successful SMEs turn satisfied customers into passionate advocates, creating a sustainable growth engine.

Remember Ganesh's words: "The day I stopped seeing my employees as workers and started seeing them as partners, everything changed. Now they don't just work for the business—they work on the business."

Are you ready to transform your team from workers to winners?

Chapter - 6

From Customers to Champions: Building Your Brand Army

"The best advertisement is a happy customer telling their friend about you."

These words from Subroto, whose educational institution now gets 70% of new business through referrals, perfectly capture the power of customer relationships.

"Customer service shouldn't just be a department,
it should be the entire company."
— *Tony Hsieh*

The Customer Revolution: Real Stories from the Ground

1. **The Feedback Transformation:** "I used to dread customer complaints," admits Arun, who runs the hospital. "Now they're our biggest source of improvement." His journey from fear to feedback is inspiring.

The Listening System:

- Regular customer surveys (simple, 3-question format)
- Feedback cards with every delivery

- Monthly customer review calls
- WhatsApp group for instant feedback
- Quick response team for complaints

"Our best-selling product came from a customer's suggestion," Nitesh shares proudly.

2. **The Technology Touch:** Mohit's retail trade business struggled with customer follow-ups until he implemented what he calls the "Connect System."

Building Customer Bonds:

- Simple CRM implementation (started with Excel, grew to proper software)
- Automated birthday/anniversary wishes
- Regular status updates
- Scheduled follow-up calls
- Customer history tracking

"Now we know exactly when to call each customer, what they prefer, and how to serve them better," Mohit explains.

3. **The Market Master:** Radha's Logistics business was losing market share until she created her "Market Intelligence Grid."

Staying Ahead:

- Weekly market trend analysis
- Competitor product monitoring
- Customer preference tracking
- Price point analysis
- Innovation opportunities identification

"We spotted a gap in the market six months before our competitors did," Radha shares. "It gave us a huge first-mover advantage."

4. **The Value Voice:** "If you don't tell your story, someone else will tell it for you," says Khushi who transformed her market position in Digital Marketing through clear communication.

   Creating Your Story:
   - Identify your unique strength
   - Document customer success stories
   - Create simple, powerful messages
   - Train team in consistent communication
   - Regular value reinforcement

5. **The Advocate Engine:** "Our customers sell for us," beams Purnendu, whose hotel hasn't spent on advertising in two years.

   Building Brand Champions:
   - Exceptional service standards
   - Regular customer appreciation events
   - Referral reward program
   - Customer success spotlights
   - Community building initiatives

The Power of Relationship: Three Success Stories

1. **The Turnaround Tale:** Amit's engineering unit was losing customers until he implemented his "Customer Connection Program":
   - Monthly customer visits
   - Quarterly review meetings

- Annual appreciation events
- Personal milestone celebrations
- Regular feedback sessions

Result: **Customer retention improved from 60% to 95% in one year.**

2. **The Growth Story:** Mohit's retail trade doubled its business through customer referrals:

- Created a customer advisory board
- Implemented feedback on products
- Started customer education programs
- Built strong after-sales support
- Developed customer community

Result: **65% of new business now comes from existing customer referrals.**

3. **The Innovation Journey:** Nitesh's Precision Parts unit created new product lines based on customer insights:

- Customer focus groups
- Product development workshops
- Market trend analysis
- Competition monitoring

Result: **Three new product lines, all successful, all customer-inspired.**

Your Action Plan

Week 1: Customer Understanding

➢ List your top 20 customers
➢ Create customer profiles

- ➤ Document their preferences
- ➤ Plan personal connect programs
- ➤ Set up feedback systems

Month 1: Technology Integration

- ➤ Choose the appropriate CRM
- ➤ Train team on usage
- ➤ Input customer data
- ➤ Set up automated reminders
- ➤ Create follow-up protocols

Quarter 1: Market Intelligence

- ➤ Start competitor analysis
- ➤ Track market trends
- ➤ Document customer feedback
- ➤ Analyse sales patterns
- ➤ Plan innovation pipeline

The Digital Advantage: "Technology is an enabler, not a replacement for relationships," reminds Vinay, whose auto components business uses technology wisely:

- ➤ WhatsApp Business for quick updates
- ➤ Simple CRM for tracking
- ➤ Email newsletters for updates
- ➤ Social media for engagement
- ➤ Online feedback systems

Looking Ahead

In our next chapter, we'll explore how to create Standard Operating Procedures (SOPs) that ensure consistent customer experience.

You'll learn how successful SMEs maintain quality while scaling their operations.

Remember Subroto's words from the beginning? He recently added: "When your customers become your salesforce, you don't just grow - you thrive."

Are you ready to turn your customers into champions?

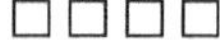

Chapter - 7

The Symphony of Systems:
Creating Your Business Orchestra

"My factory used to be like a jazz band - everyone improvising. Now it's like a symphony orchestra - everyone following the same sheet music, creating perfect harmony."

These words from Nitesh, whose precision parts unit transformed from chaos to clockwork, perfectly capture the power of systems and processes.

"Systems run the business, and people run the systems."
— *Michael Gerber*

The Systems Revolution: Real Stories from the Shop Floor

1. **The SOP Success Story:** "I was tired of explaining the same things repeatedly," shares Navneet, whose manufacturing unit struggled with inconsistent quality. Today, his unit produces identical quality across three shifts.

   Here's how:

   Building Your Process Bible:

   - Start with one critical process (Navneet began with quality checks)

- Document every step (use photos and videos)
- Test with new employees (if they can follow it, it's clear enough)
- Refine based on feedback
- Update regularly

> **"Don't make people reinvent the wheel.**
> **Give them the tools to succeed."**
> **— *David Allen***

---

2. **The Scalability Secret:** Remember Nitesh's precision parts unit? He doubled production without doubling the headcount. His secret? What he calls "The Lego Approach."

Building Blocks of Growth:
- Break processes into modules
- Standardize each module
- Create clear handoff points
- Document dependencies
- Build for expansion

"We designed every process asking one question: Will this work when we're double our size?" Nitesh explains.

3. **The Efficiency Engine:**

> **"Success is the result of perfection, hard work,**
> **learning from failure, loyalty, and persistence."**
> **— *Colin Powell***

Nitesh's precision parts unit cut waste by 10% using what he calls *"The Lean Machine."*

The Waste Warriors:

- Daily 5S practices (Sort, Set, Shine, Standardize, Sustain)
- Just-in-time inventory
- Quick changeover procedures
- Visual management boards
- Regular kaizen meetings

"Small improvements every day add up to big changes over time," Nitesh shares.

4. **The Measurement Master:**

"You can't manage what you don't measure." — ***Peter Drucker***

Deepak's steel manufacturing unit transformed after implementing his **"Numbers That Matter"** system.

Critical Numbers Dashboard:

- Production efficiency (units per hour)
- Quality metrics (defect rates)
- Delivery performance (on-time delivery %)
- Customer satisfaction scores
- Employee productivity

"Numbers tell stories that feelings can't," Deepak explains.

5. **The Quality Quest:** Vinay's auto components unit earned a reputation for zero-defect products through his "Quality First" approach.

Building Quality DNA:

➤ Clear quality standards

➤ Regular training sessions

➤ Quality circles

➤ Reward programs for zero defects

➤ Customer feedback integration

Real Transformations: Three Success Stories

1. **The Turnaround Tale:** Amit's engineering unit was drowning in customer complaints until he implemented systematic quality control through:
   - Documented procedures
   - Checkpoints at every stage
   - Regular team training
   - Quality audits
   - Customer feedback loops

   Result: Complaints dropped by 85% in six months.

2. **The Growth Story:** Raghav's labour supply business scaled from 500 to 2500 employees while maintaining quality by:
   - Modular processes
   - Clear SOPs
   - Technology integration
   - Training programs
   - Performance metrics

   Result: Output increased 5X with only a 2X staff increase.

---

3. **The Efficiency Journey:** Navneet's manufacturing unit reduced production costs by 30% by:

- Lean implementation
- Waste reduction
- Process optimization
- Energy efficiency
- Inventory management

Your Action Plan

Week 1: Process Documentation

- ➤ Choose one critical process
- ➤ Document current steps
- ➤ Identify inefficiencies
- ➤ Create simple SOP
- ➤ Test and refine

Month 1: Measurement System

- ➤ Define key metrics
- ➤ Set up tracking systems
- ➤ Create visual dashboards
- ➤ Train team on monitoring
- ➤ Start daily reviews

Quarter 1: Efficiency Drive

- ➤ Implement 5S
- ➤ Start lean practices
- ➤ Reduce waste
- ➤ Optimize workflows
- ➤ Measure improvements

Common Pitfalls to Avoid:

➢ Making processes too complex

➢ Trying to change everything at once

➢ Ignoring team feedback

➢ Focusing on paper over practice

➢ Neglecting regular updates

Technology Tools That Work

"Technology should simplify, not complicate," reminds Vinay, whose unit uses:

➢ Simple ERP system

➢ Quality control apps

➢ Digital checklists

➢ Performance dashboards

➢ Communication platforms

Looking Ahead

In our next chapter, we'll explore how visionary leadership can accelerate your transformation journey.

You'll learn how successful SME owners inspire their teams to embrace systematic thinking and drive continuous improvement.

Reflecting on Nitesh's earlier words, he recently shared" "The best part isn't just the improved efficiency - it's watching my team perform like a well-rehearsed orchestra, each person playing their part perfectly."

Are you ready to create your business symphony?

Chapter - 8

The Heartbeat of Success: Leading with Vision

"I used to be a manager running a business. Now I'm a leader building a legacy."

These words from Deepak, whose steel manufacturing unit grew from a small operation to a regional powerhouse, capture the essence of visionary leadership.

"Vision without action is a daydream.
Action without vision is a nightmare."
— Japanese Proverb

The Leadership Journey: Real Stories of Transformation

1. **The Vision Architect:** "My team used to ask 'what to do.' Now they ask 'how can we do it better?'" shares Deepak, whose steel manufacturing unit transformed through what he calls "Purpose-Driven Leadership."

Creating Your Vision Blueprint:

- Define your purpose (beyond profit)
- Paint the future picture

- Break it into milestones
- Communicate consistently
- Lead by example

"I spent one full day just imagining where we could be in five years," Deepak recalls. "That clarity changed everything."

2. **The Culture Creator:** Remember Arun? His hospital was struggling with high staff turnover until he implemented his "Leadership Ladder" approach.

   Building Leadership DNA:
   - Regular leadership training
   - Mentorship programs
   - Decision-making authority
   - Growth opportunities
   - Recognition systems

   "When people see a future for themselves, they create a future for others," Arun explains.

3. **The Change Champion:** "Change is like steering a ship," says Amit, whose engineering unit successfully navigated a major market shift. "The captain needs to be both firm and flexible."

   Managing Change:
   - Clear communication
   - Team involvement
   - Milestone celebrations
   - Regular feedback
   - Adaptive planning

"During our digital transformation, we lost no employees because everyone understood why we needed to change," Amit proudly shares.

4. **The Values Guardian:** "Values aren't posters on walls - they're decisions in action," states Radha, whose logistics business' reputation for integrity attracts premium clients.

Living Your Values:

- Define core principles

- Demonstrate through actions

- Hire for values fit

- Recognize value-aligned behavior

- Regular value discussions

"One day, we turned down a large order because it compromised our quality values. That decision earned us more respect - and more business - than any marketing could."

Three Leadership Transformations

1. **The Trust Builder:** Deepak's steel manufacturing unit struggled with micromanagement until he embraced "Trust-Based Leadership":
   - Delegated key decisions
   - Focused on outcomes
   - Provided resources
   - Accepted mistakes
   - Celebrated initiatives

Result: Productivity increased by 40% in six months.

---

2. **The Team Developer:** Amit's engineering services company created a leadership pipeline:
   - Internal training academy
   - Cross-functional exposure
   - Project leadership roles
   - Mentorship programs
   - Career progression paths

Result: **80% of supervisory positions were filled internally.**

3. **The Vision Carrier:** Arun's Hospital aligned everyone with the company vision:
   - Monthly vision meetings
   - Success story sharing
   - Goal visualization exercises
   - Progress celebrations
   - Future planning sessions

Your Leadership Development Plan

Week 1: Vision Clarity

➢ Write your purpose statement

➢ Define 5-year goals

➢ Create milestone markers

➢ Draft communication plan

➢ Share with key team members

Month 1: Culture Building

➢ Define core values

➢ Start leadership training

➢ Implement mentorship

- ➤ Create feedback channels
- ➤ Recognition program launch

Quarter 1: Change Management

- ➤ Identify needed changes
- ➤ Create change roadmap
- ➤ Communicate plans
- ➤ Train change champions
- ➤ Monitor progress

The Leadership Toolkit

"Leadership tools should empower, not control," reminds Vinay. His essential tools:

- ➤ Vision Board
- ➤ Values Charter
- ➤ Leadership Journal
- ➤ Team feedback system
- ➤ Growth tracking dashboard

Common Leadership Pitfalls:

- ➤ Confusing authority with leadership
- ➤ Focusing on short-term gains over long-term vision
- ➤ Neglecting team development
- ➤ Inconsistent communication
- ➤ Resisting change

Looking Ahead

In our next chapter, we'll explore how visionary leadership translates into financial success.

You'll learn how successful SME owners ensure their businesses remain profitable while scaling.

Building on Deepak's opening remarks, he went on to say: "The true measure of leadership isn't in the products we make or the profits we earn - it's in the leaders we create."

Are you ready to transform from a manager into a visionary leader?

The Leadership Challenge

Before we move on, take a moment to reflect:

➢ What kind of leader do you want to be?

➢ What's your vision for your business?

➢ How will you develop your team's leadership potential?

Chapter - 9

The Money Map:
Charting Your Financial Success

"I used to look at my bank balance to know how my business was doing. Now I read my business's story through its numbers."

These words from Vinay, whose auto parts unit transformed from financial stress to systematic success, perfectly capture the power of financial management.

> "Money is a tool. Used properly, it makes something beautiful; used wrong, it makes a mess."
> — *Brad Paisley*

The Financial Revolution: Real Stories of Transformation

1. **The Numbers Navigator:** "I was flying blind," admits Arun, the hospital owner. "Now every decision is backed by data." His journey from financial confusion to clarity is inspiring.

   Building Your Financial Dashboard:
   - Daily cash position tracking
   - Weekly receivables review
   - Monthly profit analysis
   - Quarterly trend evaluation
   - Annual growth planning

"Numbers tell you where you've been and show you where you can go," Arun shares.

2. The Cash Flow Master:

> **"Revenue is vanity. Profit is sanity. Cash flow is reality."**
> **— *Anonymous***

Remember Amit's engineering unit? He turned around his cash crunch using what he calls the "Cash Flow Triangle."

Managing Money Movement:

➤ Receivables acceleration

➤ Payables optimization

➤ Inventory management

➤ Credit terms negotiation

➤ Cash reserve building

"We went from struggling to pay salary to having six months of reserves," Amit beams.

3. The Growth Architect:

> **"Growth is never by mere chance; it is the result of forces working together."**
> **— *James Cash Penney***

Radha's Logistics business doubled in size without debt through her "Profitable Growth System."

The Growth Formula:

➤ Clear financial targets

➤ Reinvestment planning

➤ Cost optimization

- Efficiency monitoring

- Risk management

"Every rupee of profit had a purpose in our growth plan," Radha explains.

4. The Profit Engineer:

> "It's not how much money you make, but
> how much money you keep."
> — *Robert Kiyosaki*

Deepak's steel manufacturing unit transformed its margins through what he calls "Profit Mining."

The Profit Boosters:

- Product profitability analysis

- Cost center management

- Pricing optimization

- Waste reduction

- Efficiency improvements

Three Financial Transformations

1. **The Working Capital Wonder:** Mohit's retail trade eliminated cash flow stress:

   - Automated billing systems
   - Supplier term optimization
   - Inventory reduction
   - Credit policy revision
   - Cash flow forecasting

Result: **Working capital needs reduced by 40%.**

---

2. **The Scaling Success:** Subroto's educational institution funded expansion internally:
    - Profit reinvestment plan
    - Cost control measures
    - Technology investment
    - Process automation
    - Market expansion

Result: 100% growth in three years with zero debt.

3. **The System Builder:**

    "Do not save what is left after spending; instead, spend what is left after saving." — Warren Buffett

Arun's hospital created financial stability through systems:
    - Budgeting process
    - Expense tracking
    - Profit allocation
    - Investment planning
    - Performance monitoring

Your Financial Action Plan

Week 1: Financial Clarity

➢ Set up a basic accounting system

➢ Create daily cash tracking

➢ Separate personal/business accounts

➢ List all receivables/payables

➢ Start expense monitoring

Month 1: Profit Enhancement

➢ Analyse product profitability

➢ Review pricing strategy

➢ Identify cost-saving opportunities

➢ Set profit targets

➢ Create reinvestment plan

Quarter 1: Growth Foundation

➢ Build cash reserves

➢ Optimize working capital

➢ Plan strategic investments

➢ Set growth targets

➢ Create financial projections

The Financial Toolkit

"Simple tools used well beat complex systems used poorly," says Vinay. His essentials:

➢ Accounting software

➢ Cash flow tracker

➢ Profitability calculator

➢ Budget planner

➢ Financial dashboard

Common Financial Pitfalls:

➢ Mixing personal and business finances

➢ Ignoring cash flow for profits

➢ Undercapitalizing growth

➢ Poor receivables management

➢ Inadequate financial records

Looking Ahead

In our next chapter, we'll explore how to build a scalable business model that balances growth with stability.

You'll learn how successful SME owners create sustainable expansion while maintaining profitability.

Remember Vinay's words? He further added: "Financial management isn't about restricting growth - it's about enabling smart growth. Every number in our reports now guides our next step forward."

The Financial Challenge

Before moving on, ask yourself:

➢ Do you know your exact cash position today?

➢ What's your most profitable product or service?

➢ How many months of reserves do you have?

➢ What's your plan for funding growth?

Are you ready to transform your financial management from reactive to proactive?

❑ ❑ ❑ ❑

Chapter - 10

Building Your Growth Machine:
The Art of Scaling Smart

"My business used to be like a small shop. Today it runs like a well-oiled machine across three locations."

These words from Amit, whose engineering unit transformed from a single-location workshop to a multi-city operation, capture the essence of scalable business models.

"A business model describes the rationale of how an organization creates, delivers, and captures value."
— *Alexander Osterwalder*

The Scaling Stories: Real Transformations

1. The Revenue Diversifier:

"Do not put all your eggs in one basket." — *Warren Buffett*

"I was completely dependent on one product and three major clients," shares Nitesh, whose Precision parts unit now has multiple revenue streams. Here's how he diversified:

The Growth Matrix:

➢ Added complementary products

➢ Introduced value-added services

- ➢ Expanded geographic reach

- ➢ Developed new market segments

- ➢ Created multiple sales channels

"When one stream slows down, others keep us growing," Nitesh explains.

2. The Partnership Builder:

"If you want to go fast, go alone. If you
want to go far, go together."
*— **African Proverb***

Remember Amit's engineering unit? He doubled his market reach through what he calls "The Alliance Strategy."

Building Strong Partnerships with:

- ➢ Local service providers

- ➢ Complementary manufacturers

- ➢ Distribution networks

- ➢ Technical collaborators

- ➢ Marketing allies

"By partnering with other manufacturers, we entered five new markets without opening a single office," Amit shares.

3. The Efficiency Expert:

"Efficiency is doing things right;
effectiveness is doing the right things."
*— **Peter Drucker***

Navneet's manufacturing unit maintained quality while tripling production through his "Scale Smart System."

The Efficiency Engine:

➢ Streamlined operations

➢ Clear quality benchmarks

➢ Regular team training

➢ Performance monitoring

➢ Cost optimization

Three Real-World Scaling Success Stories

1. **The Market Expander:** Rahul's furniture manufacturing unit transformed from local to regional as he:
   - Introduced modular office furniture
   - Targeted corporate clients
   - Established showroom partnerships
   - Created installation services
   - Developed maintenance contracts

Result: **Revenue doubled in three years with higher margins.**

2. **The Systems Builder:** Amit's engineering services company scaled through smart processes using:
   - **Documented procedures**
   - **Quality control systems**
   - **Team development program**
   - **Technology integration**
   - **Performance metrics**

Result: **Handling 3X the projects with only 2X the staff.**

3. The Growth Champion:

"Growth is painful. Change is painful. But nothing is as painful as staying stuck where you do not belong." — N.R. Narayana Murthy

Vinay's auto components unit managed rapid growth while maintaining quality by:

- Systematic expansion
- Strategic hiring
- Process automation
- Quality assurance
- Culture preservation

Your Scaling Action Plan

Week 1: Revenue Diversification

➢ List potential new products/services

➢ Identify target markets

➢ Analyze competition

➢ Assess resource requirements

➢ Set growth targets

Month 1: Partnership Development

➢ Identify potential partners

➢ Create collaboration proposals

➢ Draft clear agreements

➢ Define shared objectives

➢ Launch pilot projects

Quarter 1: Efficiency Enhancement

➢ Document core processes

➢ Implement quality controls

➢ Train team members

➢ Monitor key metrics

➢ Optimize operations

Common Scaling Pitfalls:

➢ Growing too fast without systems

➢ Neglecting core business

➢ Underestimating resource needs

➢ Poor partnership agreements

➢ Compromising on quality

The Scaling Toolkit

"Tools should support growth, not complicate it," reminds Vinay. His essentials:

➢ Growth planning template

➢ Partnership evaluation checklist

➢ Quality control system

➢ Performance dashboards

➢ Resource planning tools

Handling Growth Challenges

1. **Cash Flow Management:** "We almost grew ourselves out of business," admits Ganesh, whose real estate business learned to balance growth with cash flow:

➢ Phased expansion plans

➢ Working capital optimization

- ➢ Credit line arrangements

- ➢ Customer payment terms

- ➢ Vendor negotiations

2. **Quality Control:** "Growth means nothing if quality suffers," says Arun. His solution:

- ➢ Quality checkpoints

- ➢ Staff training programs

- ➢ Regular audits

- ➢ Customer feedback systems

- ➢ Continuous improvement

3. **Culture Preservation** "Culture eats strategy for breakfast," quotes Amit, who maintained his company's values while growing:

- ➢ Regular team meetings

- ➢ Clear communication

- ➢ Value reinforcement

- ➢ Employee engagement

- ➢ Leadership development

Looking Ahead

In our next chapter, we'll explore how artificial intelligence and technology can accelerate your scaling journey.

You'll learn how successful SME owners leverage modern tools to build sustainable competitive advantages.

Remember Amit's words from our opening? He recently added: "The secret isn't just in growing bigger - it's in growing smarter. Every system we build today becomes the foundation for tomorrow's growth."

The Scaling Challenge Before moving on, ask yourself:

➤ Is your business model truly scalable?

➤ What new revenue streams could you explore?

➤ Which partnerships could accelerate your growth?

➤ Are your systems ready for expansion?

Are you ready to build your growth machine?

□ □ □ □

Chapter - 11

Riding the AI Wave:
Future-Proofing Your Business

"Will AI take my job?" This is a question I face very often.

"No, AI by itself will not take your job, but a person using AI will for sure take your job or, for that matter, even your business if you don't use AI" is my answer not just to employees but even Business Owners.

"I believe AI is going to change the world more than anything
in the history of humanity. More than electricity."
— *Kai-Fu Lee*

The Tech Revolution: Real Stories from the Ground

1. **The AI Pioneer:** "I was skeptical about AI until I saw my competitor's chatbot handling customer queries 24/7," shares Seema, whose Agro unit now leads in digital innovation. Here's her journey:

The Digital Transformation Path:

- Started with basic automation (billing, inventory)
- Added AI-powered chatbot for customer service
- Implemented predictive inventory management
- Used data analytics for decision-making
- Integrated cloud-based operations

"Now technology handles routine tasks while we focus on growth," Seema explains.

2. The Data Master:

> "AI will transform industries by amplifying human ingenuity."
> — *Satya Nadella*

Remember Vinay's auto components unit? He revolutionized his business using what he calls the **"Smart Data System."**

Leveraging Technology:

- Cloud-based operations management
- AI-powered quality control
- Predictive maintenance
- Customer behavior analysis
- Automated inventory management

"Our AI system predicted a supply shortage two months before it happened. We prepared while others struggled," Vinay shares.

3. The Digital Transformer:

> "Data is a precious thing and will last
> longer than the systems themselves."
> — *Tim Berners-Lee*

Navneet's manufacturing unit cut costs by 15% through smart technology adoption:

The Tech Toolkit:

- Power BI for data visualization
- AI-powered demand forecasting

- Automated quality checks
- Digital supply chain management
- Cloud-based collaboration

Three Client Tech Success Stories

1. **The Efficiency Champion:** Deepak's steel manufacturing unit transformed through technology:
   - Automated order processing
   - ML-powered quality control
   - Predictive maintenance
   - Digital inventory management
   - AI-enhanced customer service

Result: **40% reduction in operational costs.**

2. **The Customer Experience Master:**

   "Generative AI has the potential to unlock new forms of expression and creativity that were previously impossible."
   — *Sam Altman*

   Amit's engineering services company revolutionized service delivery:
   - AI chatbot implementation
   - Automated quote generation
   - Predictive project planning
   - Digital documentation
   - Cloud-based project management

Result: **Customer response time reduced from days to minutes.**

3. **The Data Strategist:**

   "The greatest danger in times of turbulence is not the turbulence—it is to act with yesterday's logic." — *Peter Drucker*

Nitesh's precision parts unit used data to drive growth:

- Customer behavior analysis
- Predictive analytics
- Automated reporting
- Performance tracking
- Market trend analysis

Your Technology Action Plan

Week 1: Digital Assessment

- Audit current technology usage
- Identify pain points
- Research AI solutions
- List priority areas
- Set implementation goals

Month 1: First Implementation

- Choose one key process to automate
- Train team members
- Monitor results
- Gather feedback
- Adjust as needed

Quarter 1: Advanced Integration

- Implement AI solutions
- Connect systems
- Analyze data
- Measure ROI
- Plan next steps

Handling Tech Challenges

1. The Security Shield:

> "Technology is nothing. What's important is
> that you have faith in people."
> — *Steve Jobs*

Arun's hospital created robust data protection by:

➤ Cybersecurity protocols

➤ Regular backups

➤ Access controls

➤ Employee training

➤ Incident response plans

2. The Change Champion: Deepak's steel manufacturing unit managed technology transition through:

➤ Clear communication

➤ Phased implementation

➤ Regular training

➤ Success celebrations

➤ Continuous support

3. The Cost Controller: Smart technology adoption without breaking the bank:

➤ Start with essential tools

➤ Use scalable solutions

➤ Choose cloud-based options

➤ Measure ROI regularly

➤ Upgrade strategically

Looking Ahead

In our next chapter—

We'll explore how to manage resistance to change and ensure smooth transitions as you implement these technological advancements.

Remember Vinay's words? He recently added: "The best technology isn't the most expensive - it's the one that solves your specific problems while preparing you for future challenges."

The Technology Challenge

Before moving on, ask yourself:

➢ Which processes could AI automate?

➢ What data are you not utilizing?

➢ How could technology improve customer experience?

➢ Are you ready for the digital future?

Are you ready to ride the AI wave?

☐ ☐ ☐ ☐

Chapter - 12

Embracing Change:
From Resistance to Renaissance

"My biggest competitor wasn't another business - it was the phrase 'We've always done it this way."

These words from Amit, whose engineering unit transformed from traditional to cutting-edge, capture the challenge of change management perfectly.

"Change is the law of life. And those who look only to the past or present are certain to miss the future."
— *John F. Kennedy*

The Change Champions: Real Stories of Transformation

1. The People Partner:

"People don't resist change; they resist being changed."
— *Peter Senge*

"My employees saw automation as a threat until we made them part of the solution," shares Arun, whose hospital successfully digitized operations. His approach:

The Trust Builder:

- Open communication sessions
- Employee involvement in planning
- Skills upgrade programs
- Clear growth paths
- Regular feedback meetings

"Now our team suggests changes before we do," Arun beams.

2. The Stakeholder Whisperer:

**"Great things in business are never done by one person;
they're done by a team of people."**
— Steve Jobs

Remember Amit's engineering unit? He transformed resistance into support through what he calls **"The Alliance Approach."**

Building support:

- Clear business case presentations
- Early stakeholder engagement
- Regular progress updates
- Success celebrations
- Continuous dialogue

"When our suppliers saw how digital payments improved cash flow, they became our biggest change advocates," Mohit shares.

3. The Change Architect:

**"Progress is impossible without change, and those who cannot
change their minds cannot change anything."**
— George Bernard Shaw

Radha's Logistics business implemented change systematically through her **"Smart Switch System"**:

The Change Formula:

- Pilot projects
- Phased implementation
- Regular training
- Performance monitoring
- Continuous feedback

Three Change-Management Success Stories

1. **The Culture Creator:** Deepak's steel manufacturing unit transformed workplace culture by introducing:
   - Innovation rewards
   - Learning opportunities
   - Open-door policy
   - Success sharing
   - Change champions program

   Result: **Employee suggestions led to a 30% efficiency improvement.**

2. **The Communication Master:** Amit's engineering services company managed change through clarity:
   - **Regular town halls**
   - **One-on-one sessions**
   - **Digital updates**
   - **Feedback channels**
   - **Progress tracking**

   Result: **Zero attrition during major technology upgrades.**

> ### 3. The Fear Fighter:
>
> ***"Change is the end result of all true learning." — Leo Buscaglia***
>
> Vinay's auto components unit overcame fear through education:
>
> - **Skills assessment**
> - **Customized training**
> - **Mentorship program**
> - **Career planning**
> - Recognition system

Your Change Management Plan

Week 1: Change Preparation

➢ Identify key changes needed

➢ List potential resistances

➢ Plan communication strategy

➢ Create support system

➢ Set realistic timelines

Month 1: Implementation Launch

➢ Start pilot project

➢ Gather initial feedback

➢ Make adjustments

➢ Celebrate early wins

➢ Build momentum

Quarter 1: Culture Building

➢ Establish change processes

➢ Train change champions

➢ Monitor progress

> Address concerns

> Share success stories

Common Change Pitfalls:

> Forcing change too quickly

> Poor communication

> Ignoring employee concerns

> Lack of training support

> Insufficient follow-up

The Change Toolkit

"Tools support change, but people drive it," reminds Vinay. His essentials:

> Communication templates

> Training programs

> Feedback systems

> Progress trackers

> Recognition framework

Making Change Stick

1. **The Communication Champion:** Radha's Logistics unit maintained momentum through:

    - Regular updates

    - Success stories

    - Challenge discussions

    - Solution sharing

    - Progress celebration

2. **The Skills Builder:** "Knowledge reduces fear," says Arun, who transformed his hospital through:

- Skills assessment
- Training programs
- Practice sessions
- Performance support
- Growth opportunities

3. **The Culture Curator:** Creating a change-ready culture through:

- Innovation rewards
- Learning opportunities
- Open communication
- Success sharing
- Continuous improvement

Looking Ahead

In our next chapter—

We'll explore the complete roadmap for transforming your Small and Medium Enterprise into a Systematically Managed Enterprise.

Remember Amit's words? He recently added: "The biggest change wasn't in our processes or technology - it was in our mindset. Once that shifted, everything else followed."

The Change Challenge

Before moving on, ask yourself:

➢ Where do you face the most resistance?

➢ How do you communicate change?

➢ Are you supporting your team enough?

➢ Is your culture ready for transformation?

Are you ready to turn resistance into a renaissance?

Chapter - 13

The Transformation Blueprint: Your Journey from Small to Systematic

"I used to own a business. Now I lead an institution."

These words from Vinay, whose manufacturing unit evolved from a family business to a professional enterprise, capture the essence of true transformation.

The 10 Steps to Systematic Success: Real Stories from the Ground

1. **The Vision Voyager:**

    "A vision without a plan is just a dream. A plan without a vision is just drudgery."

    "We wrote our vision statement on a tea shop napkin," shares Amit, whose engineering unit now serves three states. "Today it's on our factory wall, but more importantly, it's in our team's hearts."

    Creating Your North Star:

    -   Define your purpose
    -   Set clear goals
    -   Share the vision
    -   Live the values
    -   Inspire action

2. **The Business Auditor:** Remember Vinay's auto components unit? His transformation began with what he calls "The Mirror Test":

The Audit Checklist:

- Operations review
- Financial health check
- Market position analysis
- Technology assessment
- Team capability mapping

"What we learned in one week of honest assessment saved us years of mistakes," Amit reflects.

3. **The Structure Builder:** Radha's Logistics business transformed through systematic organization:

The Organization Blueprint:

- Clear roles and responsibilities
- Documented procedures
- Reporting systems
- Training programs
- Performance metrics

"When I took a month's vacation, the business ran better than when I was there," Radha laughs.

4. **The Operations Optimizer:**

"Excellence is not an act but a habit."

Deepak's steel manufacturing unit achieved operational excellence through:

- Process mapping
- Waste elimination

- Quality controls
- Automation
- Continuous improvement

Result: **Productivity is up by 40%, costs down by 25%.**

5. **The Financial Architect:** Amit's engineering services company built financial strength through:
   - Robust accounting systems
   - Real-time monitoring
   - Working capital optimization
   - Strategic investments
   - Risk management

6. **The Tech Transformer:** Seema's Agro unit leveraged technology for growth:
   - ERP implementation
   - CRM automation
   - Digital marketing
   - E-commerce integration
   - Data analytics

7. **The Culture Creator:** Deepak's steel manufacturing unit built a winning culture by:
   - Value alignment
   - Open communication
   - Employee recognition
   - Skills development
   - Innovation rewards

8. **The Scale Master:** Rajiv's chemical unit created a scalable model through:

- Standardized processes
- Strategic partnerships
- Market testing
- Innovation focus
- Quality consistency

9. **The Performance Monitor:**

   "What gets measured gets managed."

   Arun's hospital transformed through metrics:
   - KPI tracking
   - Regular reviews
   - Market analysis
   - Customer feedback
   - Team performance

10. **The Change Leader -The final piece:** Your leadership transformation:
    - Strategic thinking
    - Team empowerment
    - System focus
    - Innovation mindset
    - Continuous learning

Your Transformation Action Plan

Month 1: Foundation

➢ Write your vision statement

➢ Conduct business audit

➢ Map current processes

➤ Assess financial health

➤ List technology needs

Quarter 1: Structure Building

➤ Create organization chart

➤ Document procedures

➤ Implement basic systems

➤ Train key team members

➤ Set up monitoring tools

Year 1: Full Implementation

➤ Roll out all systems

➤ Build strong culture

➤ Leverage technology

➤ Scale operations

➤ Monitor and adjust

The Transformation Toolkit: Essential Tools for Your Journey:

➤ Vision document template

➤ Process mapping tools

➤ Financial dashboards

➤ Performance metrics

➤ Training programs

Success Markers: How Do You Know You're Succeeding?

➤ Systems run smoothly

➤ Team works independently

➤ Finances are stable

➤ Growth is sustainable

➤ Culture is strong

Looking Ahead

In our final chapter—

We'll explore how to sustain and build upon your transformation, ensuring your Systematically Managed Enterprise continues to grow and thrive.

Remember Vinay's words? He recently added: "The beauty of systematic management isn't just in what it does for your business - it's in what it does for your life. I now have time to dream bigger because my systems handle the present while I plan the future."

The Transformation Challenge

Before moving on, ask yourself:

➤ Is your vision clear and compelling?

➤ Are your systems ready for growth?

➤ Is your team aligned with your goals?

➤ Are you ready to lead this change?

Are you ready to transform your business from small to systematic?

☐ ☐ ☐ ☐

Chapter - 14

Your Living Legacy:
Building Beyond Business

"Success isn't just about what you accomplish in your life - it's about what you inspire others to do."

These powerful words from Deepak, whose transformed manufacturing unit now mentors dozens of budding entrepreneurs, capture the essence of true legacy building.

Beyond Profits: Real Stories of Impact

1. **The Community Builder:** "I realized my true success wasn't in my bank balance, but in the lives we touched," shares Seema, whose Agro unit has become a catalyst for rural development.

    Creating Lasting Impact:
    - Youth training programs
    - Farmer support initiatives
    - Environmental projects
    - Community education
    - Local entrepreneurship support

    "We don't just grow vegetables anymore - we nurture dreams," Seema explains.

2. **The Future Architect:** Remember Amit's engineering unit? He built sustainability into every aspect through what he calls "The Legacy Framework":

Building for Tomorrow:

- Succession planning
- Innovation investments
- Environmental initiatives
- Community engagement
- Knowledge sharing

"When my daughter chose to join the business, I knew we'd built something worth continuing," Amit shares.

3. **The Mentor Movement:** "The best way to predict the future is to create it."

Navneet's manufacturing unit transformed local entrepreneurship through:

- Business incubation programs
- Skill development workshops
- Startup mentoring
- Resource sharing
- Networking events

Three Legacy Stories

1. **The Social Innovator:** Deepak's steel manufacturing unit revolutionized waste management:

   - Recycling initiatives
   - Community awareness
   - Green technology adoption
   - Zero-waste programs
   - Environmental education

   Result: Created a model other industries now follow.

---

2. **The Knowledge Sharer:** Amit's engineering company built an education ecosystem:

Technical training center

- **Student internships**
- **Industry partnerships**
- **Research collaboration**
- **Innovation labs**

Result: Trained over 100 young engineers.

3. **The Global Connector:** "Think locally, act globally." Deepak's steel manufacturing unit created an international impact:

Export excellence

- **Global standards**
- **Cross-border partnerships**
- **Technology transfer**
- Knowledge exchange

Your Legacy Action Plan

Month 1: Foundation Building

- Define your legacy vision
- Identify impact areas
- Plan community initiatives
- Set sustainability goals
- Design mentorship programs

Year 1: Impact Creation

- Launch CSR projects
- Start mentoring programs
- Build partnerships

➢ Document journey

➢ Measure outcomes

Decade 1: Legacy Establishment

➢ Scale successful programs

➢ Create institutions

➢ Build knowledge bases

➢ Develop future leaders

➢ Expand influence

The Legacy Toolkit

Essential elements for lasting impact:

➢ Succession plans

➢ CSR frameworks

➢ Training programs

➢ Documentation systems

➢ Impact metrics

Creating Sustainable Impact

1. **The Environment Champion:** Deepak's steel manufacturing unit led green initiatives:
   - Solar power adoption
   - Water conservation
   - Waste reduction
   - Green supply chain
   - Environmental education

2. **The Next-Gen Builder:** "Leadership is about making others better as a result of your presence and making sure that impact lasts in your absence."

> Arun's hospital focused on youth development:
> - Apprenticeship programs
> - Leadership training
> - Innovation challenges
> - Career guidance
> - Entrepreneurship support
>
> 3. **The Story Keeper:** Documenting and sharing success:
>   - Published case studies
>   - Regular workshops
>   - Online knowledge base
>   - Media engagement
>   - Industry forums

Final Thoughts: Your Journey Continues

Remember, true success isn't measured in quarters but in generations. As you transform your Small and Medium Enterprise into a Systematically Managed Enterprise, you're not just building a business - you're creating a legacy that will inspire and impact long after you're gone.

The Legacy Questions

Before we conclude, ask yourself:

➢ What impact do you want to create?

➢ How will your business serve society?

➢ What knowledge will you share?

➢ Who will you mentor?

➢ What stories will they tell about your journey?

As Deepak recently reflected: "Twenty years ago, I wanted to build a successful business. Today, I know that success without significance is meaningless. Build something that matters - not just to your balance sheet, but to the world."

Your journey from a Small and Medium Enterprise to a Systematically Managed Enterprise is just the beginning. The real adventure lies in using this platform to create lasting, positive change in your community and beyond.

Are you ready to build your living legacy?

Reach out:

vikash@jainkhemka.in

Words of Praise

CA Vikash Jain's guidance in implementing professional systems, particularly his expertise in integrating AI-driven solutions, has helped Gagan Group evolve with changing times. His practical approach bridges traditional business wisdom with modern technology, enabling us to build efficient, scalable processes. For SMEs aiming to stay competitive in today's digital age, his insights into systematic management and technology adoption provide a valuable roadmap for transformation.

Vinay Agarwal
CMD, Gagan Ferrotech Ltd.

Wisdom is a boundless treasure, manifesting itself in the words of friends, the guidance of elders, the insights of mentors, the influence of visionaries, and, most profoundly, in the depths of our own experiences. Yet, its unstructured flow often renders it cumbersome to translate into actionable steps.

SME to SME: Journey from being a Small and Medium Enterprise to a Systematically Managed Enterprise by CA Vikash Kumar Jain offers a masterfully curated framework that not only captivates the reader but systematically addresses the inevitable challenges and detours one encounters on this transformative path.

The book's pragmatic lens, combined with its strategic narrative, makes it a must-read for leaders aspiring to achieve sustainable growth and mental clarity. Kudos to the author for crafting such an insightful guide!

Deepak Chowdhury

President-Commercial, Shyam Steel Industries Ltd.

For two decades, Vikash Ji has been more than just our Chartered Accountant at Allied Iron Products Pvt Ltd-he's been our compass and confidant. His expertise helped transform us from a small local business into an export-oriented company.

Through countless industry changes and evolving government regulations, he has been our constant, ensuring we stayed informed and prepared. Beyond the numbers, he's been a true friend and mentor, touching the lives of everyone from leadership to our accounting staff with his kindness and wisdom.

Words cannot express the depth of our gratitude for his belief in us and his commitment to our growth. He is truly a blessing to our journey.

Best of Luck for the Future and Keep Growing in Life & Always remember:

"Growth in life is not just about reaching new heights but about lifting others along the way. True success lies in the wisdom shared, the kindness shown, and the lives inspired."

Nitesh Jain

CEO-Allied Iron Products Pvt Ltd